The
Connell Guide
to

———————

How to Read
a Poem

———————

by Malcolm Hebron
with
Andrew Hodgson and Caroline Moore

Contents

Introduction

This book is written with one aim: to help you read, understand and appreciate poetry. The English language has an extraordinarily rich stock of poems to its credit, from the epic *Beowulf*, written perhaps as early as the eighth century, to the poetry of Simon Armitage, Carol Ann Duffy and the many other fine writers working today.

And all this wonderful stock is there to be *read*. Do you really need a guide to that? Can't you just get on and read it? You certainly can. But there is some stuff you just have to know if you are going to get the most out of it. Reading poetry *well* is something I am still learning to do, and in this book I pass on where I have got up to so far.

Listening to ghosts

I've never seen a ghost. But there's a house I know in Devon which used to be a barn. One day the owner went downstairs and found a man standing there, in Victorian clothes. He was just standing, lost in thought, in the middle of the kitchen. After a time, without a word, the visitor left.

So I'm quite willing to accept there may be ghosts out there. I've just never seen one myself. But I have, in one way, had many meetings with the dead, and you have, too: through reading books.

It's easy to forget what strange things books *are*. The shelf I'm looking at, right now, holds the words of human beings from all sorts of times and places: just by opening these volumes, I can let their voices flood into my mind. I can share the experiences of a soldier in the First World War, listen to someone who was in love in the 16th century, lose myself in a story that takes me to the taverns of 17th-century Spain.

Through their writings, authors from different ages, and all sorts of different places, have sent their experiences out into the world where, miraculously, they have survived, while the writers themselves have lived their lives and passed on. And the most distilled, intense record they have left us is to be found in poetry.

Let's go back to my ghost story from Devon. But now imagine it's *you* who goes downstairs. There in front of you, in flickering candlelight, is an old man, dressed in Victorian clothes. He has white hair. He leans on a stick. The room is quite bare, but there's a tall mirror in front of him. He stares into it for a while. You stand, transfixed. Then he starts speaking – to you, or to himself? Has he even seen you? It's hard to tell. His voice is quiet, almost a whisper.

This is what he says:

> *I look into my glass,*
> *And view my wasting skin*
> *And say, 'Would God it came to pass*
> *My heart had shrunk as thin!'*
>
> *For then I, undistrest*
> *By hearts grown cold to me,*
> *Could lonely wait my endless rest*
> *With equanimity.*
>
> *But Time, to make me grieve,*
> *Part steals, lets part abide;*
> *And shakes this fragile frame at eve*
> *With throbbings of noontide.*

Then a long silence falls. The candle sputters and goes out. Not knowing how, you find yourself outside. But the words of the old man stay with you.

I'm getting old, he seemed to be saying, *my skin is wasting away, my body is frail. If only my feelings would fade away as well! Then I wouldn't mind if people felt coldly towards me, for I could just wait calmly for death to come. But no, Time won't let me off the hook. Still I feel the passions and desires that I did when I was a young man in the noon of life, surging through me. I'm old on the outside, but young on the inside, close to death yet still so alive. Why can't my feelings go away and leave me in peace?*

It's a sad thought – the shadows are lengthening... Is that what it's like being old? Some of what he says seems odd, and surprising.

And view my wasting skin...

Curious words. Why *view*, and not *see*? A *view* suggests you're having a good long look, like the view from a clifftop. And *wasting*, not *wasted*: that –*ing*, that little word ending, makes us think that the skin is wasting away, *right now, even as he looks in the mirror*.

And the *fragile frame* is presumably the man's body, yet it makes you think of some tottering wooden barn, shaken by *throbbings of noontide*, as if his feelings are like a wind or an earthquake stirring the foundations, making the whole structure creak. The poet doesn't sound as if he is feeling sorry for himself, though. His verses are delivered in a dignified, unhurried way, through lines of measured rhyming verse, with some thoughtful, educated words, such as *equanimity* (meaning calmness, or self-control). That's not how we sound when we're asking for sympathy. There is no complaint here, just a restrained statement of feeling.

For then I, undistrest...

Undistrest is another unusual word: the life the poet dreams of is one defined by its absence of distress rather than by any positive quality.

And look at that word the poem ends on: *noontide*. In the Bible noontide was associated with temptation: Christian monks used to talk about the *noontide demon*. You don't need to know this to understand the poem, but the poet clearly knew it, and his image is carefully chosen. This is a poem about a particular kind of temptation: the temptation of youthful desire and passion.

Well, that is one way of reading a poem. On this occasion you met the ghost of the poet and novelist, Thomas Hardy.

Another way of reading a poem is to see it as a *journey*. It takes us from the familiar to the strange, from the known to the unknown. In this poem, Hardy takes us on a journey from looking into a mirror – a familiar experience – to what must be for most of us the unknown, strange world of being old yet flooded with the passions of youth.

Some poems, especially from earlier history, sound rather grand, as if a wizard or prophet is speaking. A lot of modern poetry is more like someone chatting to you across the table. But in both cases – whether it's the prophet speaking, or the companion across the table – a poem makes you put other things to the back of your mind and *give the speaker your attention*.

That's what this book is about. Its aim is to give you some suggestions on how we can pay attention to poetry, and make the most of its message. "It is the business of the poet to touch our hearts by showing his own," was how Thomas Hardy put it. The pages that follow are about how to be touched. How to read a poem. How to listen to ghosts.

Section One: What?

What's it about?

"The poets have been mysteriously silent on the subject of cheese." (G K Chesterton)

When we read a poem for the first time, a useful thing to do is *to forget it's a poem*. We need to be clear *what* it is saying before we think about *how* it is saying it. (There are poems about all sorts of things though not many, as Chesterton reminds us, on the subject of cheese.)

Love and Friendship

Love is like the wild rose briar,
Friendship, like the holly tree –
The holly is dark when the rose-briar blooms
But which will bloom most constantly?

The wild rose-briar is sweet in spring,
Its summer blossoms scent the air;
Yet wait till winter comes again
And who will call the wild-briar fair?

Then scorn the silly rose-wreath now
And deck thee with the holly's sheen,
That when December blights thy brow
He still may leave thy garland green.

(Emily Bronte, 1818-1848)

In other words...

Love is like a rose, and friendship is like the holly. Next to the blooming rose, the holly seems dull. But which one would you rely on? In spring and summer, the rose is in bloom and smells lovely. But in winter it fades away. Forget about love, then, which is wonderful but short-lived, and go for friendship. Then, when your winter time comes, you still have a friend you can count on.

Or, to put it in a sentence: *romantic love is wonderful but short-lived, while friendship is permanent and won't desert you.*

You might ask: "Why didn't she just say that and save us all some time?" But Bronte has put these thoughts across in a way which is musical, which moves in pleasant rhythmic way, and gives us pictures to go with the abstract ideas. All of this helps us to remember it. Another poet, W. H. Auden, defined poetry simply as "memorable speech".

The paraphrase above is what we call the **argument** of the poem.

Once we have an idea of the argument, we can ask: "What does it make us think about?" The poem above turns our mind to love and friendship, but maybe to other things, too – how so often in life the most exciting things only last for a short time, while the most valuable ones are those we don't pay much attention to.

The subjects that a poem makes us think about are its **themes**. It's a common misconception that the ideas of poetry are deep: often they are quite simple, and familiar. But Bronte expresses what is a common idea in a vivid, striking way and in so doing she makes the familiar seem unfamiliar. Another famous remark about poetry is that it gives us (in the words of Alexander Pope) "What oft was thought but ne'er so well expressed".

Let's look at a harder poem. Emily Bronte led us by the hand and pointed out what her images meant. But not all poets do this. Sometimes they give us more work to do. Here's another poem about a rose.

The Sick Rose

O Rose thou art sick.
The invisible worm,
That flies in the night
In the howling storm:

Has found out thy bed
Of crimson joy:
And his dark secret love
Does thy life destroy.

(William Blake, 1757-1827)

Where Bronte kindly told us what the rose and holly

William Blake's hand-coloured print, presenting The Sick Rose *in his typical style*

stood for, Blake is not so considerate. So all we can do is retell the strange little story:

You're ill, rose! There's a worm, which is invisible and flies in the stormy night and it's found you in your bed and it's destroying you with its love.

So what do the rose and the worm mean? I don't know. *No one knows.* Critics and scholars still debate these mysterious eight lines. And Blake didn't help us by writing down the answer on the back. Perhaps even *he* didn't know! Maybe it was a vision or dream that he just wrote down because it felt significant to him.

A rose is associated in our minds with love, beauty, fragility (as in the previous poem). And it's clear that the worm here is something dangerous – it's invisible, it flies in a storm, it destroys with a *secret love*. Could it be one of those insects that gets into flowers and makes them ill and covered in spots? Maybe. But the poet is not writing an article for a gardening magazine. He must have bigger ideas in mind.

What, then, does the poem make us think about? Perhaps of how vulnerable, beautiful things are open to attack, how even love can be damaging. Perhaps *dark secret* suggests the wrong kind of love? When we learn that the poem is from a collection called *Songs of Innocence and Experience*, we might find that useful, too. The rose is like youthful innocence, and the worm, maybe, is the forces of experience that come for us when we grow up, that eat away our innocence. Some critics have even suggested that the poem refers to sex – the worm, the crimson bed... Perhaps they're right.

"The Sick Rose" is an example of a poem which on one level is a story of a flower and a worm. But we suspect it's really about something else, just as the fable of the hare and the tortoise isn't about the different velocity of animals but about how sure and steady wins the day over sheer speed.

Often, in poetry, things or animals or plants stand for ideas: a rose for love, holly for friendship, a worm for corruption. When used in this way, they are called **symbols**. Symbols can be an effective way of helping us understand the invisible world of ideas.

Stirring up our emotions

Poems convey *emotions* – hope, despair, defiance, love, fear. It's hard really to separate the mind and the heart. The main two uses we make of language are to say what we think and to say (or show) what we feel. Poetry brings the two together. Robert Frost puts it like this: "Poetry is when an emotion has found its thought and the thought has found words."

Here's a poem by a writer who had a lot to say about emotions, William Wordsworth.

I wandered lonely as a cloud

I wandered lonely as a cloud
That floats on high o'er vales and hills,
When all at once I saw a crowd,
A host, of golden daffodils;
Beside the lake, beneath the trees,
Fluttering and dancing in the breeze.

Continuous as the stars that shine
And twinkle on the milky way,
They stretched in never-ending line
Along the margin of a bay:
Ten thousand saw I at a glance,
Tossing their heads in sprightly dance.

The waves beside them danced; but they
Outdid the sparkling waves in glee:
A poet could not but be gay,
In such a jocund company:
I gazed – and gazed – but little thought
What wealth the show to me had brought:

For oft, when on my couch I lie
In vacant or in pensive mood,
They flash upon that inward eye
Which is the bliss of solitude;
And then my heart with pleasure fills,
And dances with the daffodils.

(William Wordsworth, 1770-1850)

This is a famous poem, but the best thing to do with a famous poem is to pretend you're the first person who's ever seen it. Imagine it's just tumbled out of a dusty box in a charity shop. Read it like that and you might be surprised. Is this about the poet in ecstasy at the beauty of daffodils? That's what we might *expect* in a poem which begins as this one does (and indeed the poem is often, wrongly, called "Daffodils").

But poets love confounding our expectations, and when we read a poem we have to be careful to attend to what it is *actually* saying.

In terms of feeling, then, what is going on? First the speaker says he *wandered lonely*. There's our first emotion word, *lonely*, but he doesn't *sound* very lonely: it comes over as a rather nice loneliness, floating freely like a cloud. Then he sees the daffodils. Look at the wonderfully inventive verbs and adverbs: *fluttering, twinkling, tossing...* They *outdid the sparkling waves in glee...* He tells us that the company of the flowers made him feel gay, in its sense of 'happy':

A poet could not but be gay...

But as he loses himself in *looking*, he doesn't think at all about the experience:

> *I gazed – and gazed – but little thought*
> *What wealth the show to me had brought.*

The sight is doing him good without his even being aware of it. It's not until the last verse that the joy catches up with him, as a delayed reaction. When he's idle and *pensive*, the daffodils come back to him as a golden memory and

> *...then my heart with pleasure fills,*
> *And dances with the daffodils.*

Far from being the word *daffodils*, that little word *then*, in the second to last line, is perhaps the most important in the poem. It is the word on which the poem turns. His heart dances with the daffodils *now*, in a way it *didn't* dance with them first time round. (*I gazed – and gazed – but little thought...*)

So the poem takes us on a much more interesting emotional journey than we might expect from the opening lines. As one of the best modern critics of Wordsworth, Seamus Perry, says, this is really a poem about "sitting on your sofa" – a poem about memory. Wordsworth is telling us that the happiest moments in life sometimes go unnoticed at the time; we're so busy living them, experiencing them, that we're not really aware of being happy, or full of wonder. Only later do these moments come back to us – as intense memories – and it is then that we feel the pleasure or wonder we didn't really feel at the time.

"Poetry is the language in which man explores his own amazement," said Christopher Fry, and it is worth noting that the word *amazement* suggests not only wonder but also bewilderment or confusion – the maze of feelings and thoughts that the poet must work through, as Wordsworth does in "I wandered lonely as a cloud".

His poem is what we call a **lyric**, the most common type of poetry nowadays. Lyrics tend to be short and compressed – little grenades of thought-feeling-words. When they are in the first person, with an "I" speaking to us, they will often tell us directly what emotions are involved: *lonely... gay... bliss... pleasure.*

But there are other kinds of poem, and emotion can be conveyed in other ways. Below is a less well-known piece, a description of a bird that perches in a crocodile's mouth and acts as an avian toothpick, pecking food from between its teeth.

The Crocodile Bird

Beside the fruitful shore of muddy Nile,
Upon a sunny bank outstretchèd lay
In monstrous length, a mighty Crocodile,
That crammed with guiltless blood, and greedy prey
Of wretched people travailling that way,
Thought all things less than his disdainful pride.
I saw a little bird, called Tedula,
The least of thousands which on earth abide,
That forced this hideous beast to open wide
The grisly gates of his devouring hell,
And let him feed, as Nature doth provide,
Upon his jaws, that with black venom swell.
Why then should greatest things the least disdain,
Since that so small so mighty can constrain?

(Edmund Spenser, 1552-1599)

In these lines Spenser gives us an interesting little tale of how a mighty monster can be controlled by a tiny bird, who forces it to open its jaws and let him peck away at the scraps. And he wraps it up with a moral: big powerful animals shouldn't think they are so great, when tiny ones can sometimes control them. He probably meant us to think about kings and popes and the common man, using the animal story to make his point. This particular kind of tale is called a **fable**.

But at the same time the poet winds us into his world on the banks of the sunny Nile by making us feel things. Horrible monster! Poor travellers! Plucky little bird! We take it all in much better if we're emotionally involved.

How does he achieve this? Look, first, at the words he uses to make the crocodile seem violent and unpleasant. *Monstrous, greedy, disdainful, hideous*. Even the bits of the crocodile, like the *black venom* on his teeth, are nasty. This kind of language is called **emotive**. Emotive language goes straight for the jugular, stirring up our feelings. Meanwhile, the bird, the *tedula*, is *little... the least of thousands*. We admire him as a cunning little chappy, forcing the mighty beast to open its jaws. Other emotive words make us feel sorry for the travellers, who are *guiltless* and *wretched*. We react not just to the **meanings** of words, but also to their **associations**. For example, *black* literally means a colour, but in the phrase *black venom* we associate it with death and evil.

The second way the poet is swaying our emotions is by the use of images. First we see the Nile as a pleasant place, with a *fruitful shore* and *sunny bank*.

Those pictures of fruit and sun conjure up a picture of a placid and fertile place. But it is spoilt by the huge monster. His mouth is pictured as *grisly gates*, leading to *devouring hell*, and his jaws drip with *black venom*.

Finally, a poet can use *sound* to nudge us into imagining the scene more vividly and getting emotionally involved. Just listen to the fantastic line

That crammed with guiltless blood, and
                              greedy prey

It's crammed itself with juicy sounds that echo the monster crunching up its victims: ***crammed, guiltless** ... **gr**eedy*. Now contrast these heavy monster sounds with the light tripping sounds around the tiny bird:

I saw a little bird, called Tedula.

Those heavy sounds come back to give us the big, dangerous *grisly gates*, and the stressed *black venom swell*. This is like background music to a film, taking our emotions this way and that.

Looking for the conflict

One helpful tip is to look for the central tension, or opposition, in a poem. The Irish poet W B Yeats said: "out of the quarrel with ourselves we make poetry". As readers, we can try to trace those quarrels in the poetry we read.

Think about the poems we have read so far. All of them are working out some kind of opposition. Hardy's poem, "I look into my glass", describes the tension between the ageing body and the still virile feelings within. Emily Bronte explores the opposition between romantic love – sensational but brief – and friendship. Blake's "The Sick Rose" is about the opposition between the rose and the worm, innocence and corruption.

The opposition in Wordsworth's poem is less obvious, but it involves a kind of tension between an event when we *experience* it and, later, when we *remember* it, a tension between the *then* and the *now*. Spenser's concern is the opposition between the mighty crocodile and the tiny bird which controls him. In each case, there's a kind of either/or – an on the one hand/on the other hand working itself out.

And what is true of these poems is true of most poetry. There is almost always an opposition – between positive and negative, good and evil, order and disorder, love and death, pleasant and unpleasant. It might be buried deep or it might be on the surface. It is often there at the start: O *Rose, thou art sick*! Beauty versus sickness. Everything follows from that.

Read this poem by Byron and see if you can find opposing words or ideas early on.

She Walks in Beauty

She walks in beauty, like the night
Of cloudless climes and starry skies;
And all that's best of dark and bright
Meet in her aspect and her eyes;
Thus mellowed to that tender light
Which heaven to gaudy day denies.

One shade the more, one ray the less,
Had half impaired the nameless grace
Which waves in every raven tress,
Or softly lightens o'er her face;
Where thoughts serenely sweet express,
How pure, how dear their dwelling-place.

And on that cheek, and o'er that brow,
So soft, so calm, yet eloquent,
The smiles that win, the tints that glow,
But tell of days in goodness spent,
A mind at peace with all below,
A heart whose love is innocent!

The central tension in this poem is there from in the very first line. It is between light and dark: she, the poet's subject, walks in *beauty*, like the *night*. It is the stars that give the night its beauty. The beautiful woman brings together the night and the stars:

*all that's best of **dark** and **bright***
Meet in her aspect, and her eyes.

She embodies a *tender light*, the day mellowed by the night. She occupies the perfect middle point; one more *shade* or one more *ray* would spoil it. The beauty is in her dark *raven* hair, and *lightens* in her face. In the final stanza this physical beauty becomes a picture of moral perfection, as light and dark give way to an other-worldly *heart whose love is innocent*. The beautiful woman herself has worked out the opposition of light and dark, forming a mysterious

AMBIGUITY

Poems are often ambiguous. It is is possible to interpret them in different ways. In his "Elegy in a County Churchyard", Thomas Gray writes:

> *Full many a gem of purest*
> *ray serene*
> *The dark, unfathomed caves*
> *of ocean bear;*
> *Full many a flower is born to*
> *blush unseen*
> *And waste its sweetness on*
> *the desert air.*

Gray is telling us that people from poor backgrounds find it difficult to be famous. He compares them to gems, hidden away in caves, and to flowers which bloom in the desert instead of being plucked and displayed in vases.

The critic William Empson, however, says that while farm labourers may *want* to escape their poverty, gems *don't mind* being hidden in caves and flowers, surely, are quite happy to be left to *blush unseen*.

Besides, the verse is so beautiful that we might feel, on reading it, that this a perfectly healthy, happy state of existence. Why would we want to see it altered? The poet is suggesting the poor should not be denied the limelight. Yet the imagery of the gems and flowers seems to be at odds with the argument it is supposed to be supporting. ∎

harmony.

Here, by way of contrast, is a poem by one of my favourite contemporary poets, Alice Oswald.

Body

This is what happened
the dead were settling in under their mud roof
and something was shuffling overhead

it was a badger treading on the thin partition

bewildered were the dead
going about their days and nights in the dark
putting their feet down carefully and finding themselves floating
but that badger

still with the simple heavy box of his body needing to be lifted
was shuffling away alive

hard at work
with the living shovel of himself
into the lane he dropped
*   not once looking up*

and missed the sight of his own corpse falling like a suitcase
*   towards him*
with the grin like an opened zip
*   (as I found it this morning)*

and went on running with that bindweed will of his

went on running along the hedge and into the earth again
trembling
as if in a broken jug for one backwards moment
water might keep its shape

(Alice Oswald, from Falling Awake)

There is so much to enjoy here, from that startling opening picture of the dead settling in, to that wonderful comparison of the badger's will to bindweed. The poem creates a rich and vivid world for us to inhabit.

Is there a controlling opposition, helping to unite the various parts? I would suggest it's a very ancient opposition between the primal forces of life and death. On the one hand we have the dead, settling down, and on the other the living badger, shuffling away, going about his badgery business.

The tension runs through the language: the dead are *putting their feet down carefully* and *floating*, and these light and ethereal actions contrast with the badger with his *heavy body*. They, the dead, are *settled down* and he is *hard at work*. The opposition works itself out in the final lines, where the badger seems to be dead and alive at the same time, perhaps in his last *backwards moment* imagining scurrying along the hedge as he crashes down into the lane, where the poet finds him later.

In "Body" the central opposition is fairly straightforward; in the famous verses which follow it is much less so.

A Red, Red Rose

O my Luve is like a red, red rose
That's newly sprung in June:
O my Luve's like a melodie,
That's sweetly played in tune.

As fair art thou, my bonnie lass,
So deep in luve am I;
And I will luve thee still, my dear,
Till a' the seas gang dry.

Till a' the seas gang dry, my dear,
And the rocks melt wi' the sun;
And I will luve thee still, my dear,
While the sands o' life shall run.

And fare-thee-weel, my only Luve!
And fare-thee-weel, a while!
And I will come again, my Luve,
Tho 'twere ten thousand mile.

(Robert Burns, 1759-1796)

This is one of the great romantic poems. Notice how Burns expresses an abstract idea by using a vivid concrete picture. His love is

like a red, red rose,
That's newly sprung in June.

That repeated *red* suggests how intense his passion

is, and the idea of the rose being newly sprung gets across his sense of delighted surprise. His beloved is like a melody, not just *sweetly played* but *in tune* as well – double bonus! But the picture of music also stirs our imagination, and gets across the idea of him taking *time* to contemplate her, as it takes time to listen to a piece of music.

Later we have the images of the sea going dry, the rocks melting with the sun – images of impossible things, emphasising how he will love her forever. But they also put the idea of the end of time, and the end of love, in our minds. If we're looking for an internal tension here, it is between the rapture of the moment and the sense that it will not last, that time marches on. The big abstract word in the poem is *Love*, but it's the concrete imagery that gives it depth and power.

The very images Burns uses suggest the tension at the heart of the poem, the tension between his knowledge that love can't last and his desperate hope that it will. In one sense that inspired word *sprung* isn't quite right: rosebushes *don't* spring up in June, they're there all year round. But roses *do* bloom in June. So the image is both natural and unnatural at the same time, both realistic and magical.

As anyone who knows about Burns's life will tell you, the truth was that he was a serial womaniser who was constantly falling in love and constantly thinking it would last for ever. But we don't need to know this biographical detail to feel the

Lord Byron (1788 – 1824)

psychological truth of the poem. Every time you fall in love you think: this is it. And though Burns knows in one part of his mind that his love won't last for ever – *"Till a' the seas gang dry"* – he passionately believes that it will. The tone of the poem is an irresistible mixture of celebration and defiance.

"Poetic language" refers to the kinds of words we might expect to meet in poetry, but not anywhere else:

> *The sun's gaudy chariot rode o'er the shining mead.*

That sort of thing. We meet such language particularly in older poetry before about 1900. A poem was formal, not casual, a sort of dinner party with words. This produces what critics call **heightened** language:

> *Ye distant spires, ye antique towers*
> *That crown the watery glade,*
> *Where grateful Science still adores*
> *Her Henry's holy shade ...*
>
> (Thomas Gray, 1716-1771,
> from "Ode on a Distant Prospect of Eton College")

This is language in evening dress. It's rather out of fashion now, but it was all the rage for Gray and his readers. The poet is doing everything possible to lift us to a lofty, golden world: archaic terms like *ye*, *antique* (pronounced ántic), and *glade*... the personified *Science*... and the long rolling sentence, itself a sign of language behaving itself in an elegant and sophisticated manner.

   Later poets have largely turned away from the poetic (and before it, too: Hardy was deliberately writing against that style). I wonder what Thomas Gray would have made of John Agard, for example:

Listen Mr Oxford Don

Me not no Oxford don
me a simple immigrant
from Clapham Common
I didn't graduate
I immigrate

(John Agard, 1949 –)

Agard is here using colloquial speech patterns from his
native Caribbean. In later verses, the speaker says he is
wanted for crimes against the English language:

... muggin' the Queen's English
is the story of my life.

The poem is making us think about what we regard as
proper and correct in language, and how those who
speak differently, perhaps because of their background,
can feel rejected by the establishment. Agard's poem is
carefully organised: notice the rhyme of *don* and
common, and the yoking together of *graduate* and
immigrate to make us reflect on how immigrants may
be deprived of education and the chances it provides.

Both Gray and Agard are writing about knowledge
and education; but while Gray is praising the
establishment in the form of Eton's spires, Agard is
having some gentle fun with the Oxford don and the
Oxford Dictionary. Their poems are like two paths, one
polished and shiny and the other a bit rougher; but they
both lead somewhere important. ■

Section Two: How?

Under the bonnet...

"Poetry is language at its most distilled and most powerful."

(Rita Dove)

To understand a car, we need to know roughly what goes on under the bonnet. It's the same with poetry. We have considered *what* poems say – their argument, themes, the emotions behind them, the tensions within them. We will now think about *how* they say what they say.

We have already looked at the way poets use words in striking and unexpected ways. What is any poem, after all, but a string of words arranged into lines? Indeed, a useful exercise if a word surprises you is to ask: how different would the effect be if the poet had used the obvious word instead? It makes you think about the word the poet *does* use – and why it is there. So we noticed, for example, that Thomas Hardy used *wasting* not *wasted* in "I look into my glass" – because *wasting* makes it seem as if the process is happening now, at this very moment.

What poetry often does is anchor big, abstract ideas in concrete language, in a world of things we can see, touch, hear or smell. In the poems we have looked at so far, a lot of the language is drawn from nature: roses, holly, worms, daffodils along a bay, starry skies, the badger. Living in towns and cities

– as most people do these days – is one of the greatest sources of difficulty for a modern reader. We are cut off from the natural world which most writers in history lived close to, and understood.

So going for a good walk in the country, and keeping your eyes peeled when you do, is probably as good a way of preparing to read literature as anything you'll read in a guide. But in the meantime let's have an under-the-bonnet look at four aspects of the *how* of poetry: imagery, sound, rhythm and structure.

1. Imagery

> *"Painting is silent poetry, and poetry is painting that speaks."* (Plutarch)

There's a phrase in Latin, *"ut pictura poesis"*, which means "poetry is like a picture". And poetry is certainly full of pictures. Opening the poetry anthology next to me at random a few times, I find these lines:

> *So all day long the noise of battle roll'd*
> *Among the mountains by the winter sea;*
> (Alfred, Lord Tennyson)

> *O Nightingale, that on yon bloomy spray*
> *Warbl'st at eve, when all the woods are still*
> (John Milton)

A region desolate and wild.
Black, chafing water: and afloat,
And lonely as a truant child
In a waste wood, a single boat.

(Matthew Arnold)

You bring them in, a trug of thundercloud,
Neglected in long grass and the sulk
Of a wet summer.

(Gillian Clarke)

That's quite a range of pictures, from the mountains by the sea in the first quotation, to the single boat on a lake, to the flowers brought in from outside. One of the most successful exercises I've ever done was to invite a class to copy out a poem and draw pictures from it on the opposite page. It may sound childish, but childish activities can take us to the fundamentals of reading, which we must take care we are not educated out of.

There are two observations I'd like to make about these images. One is that they are very *exact*. Time after time, when we look at poems, we find that the poet wants to give us something precise: not just a sea, but a *winter* sea, not just water but *black, chafing* water.

In Elizabeth Gaskell's novel, *The Cranford Chronicles*, one of the characters, Mr Holcroft, reads Tennyson's poem "The Gardener's Daughter". He realises that what really fires Tennyson's interest is not the gardener's daughter, but the garden.

Tennyson describes

> those eyes
> *Darker than darkest pansies, and that hair*
> *More black than ashbuds in the front of*
> *March.*

The image sends Mr Holbrook out into the garden to check. Is Tennyson right? Are ashbuds in March *really* black? And he discovers to his surprise that, yes, they are. Tennyson is right. "And I've lived all my life in the country; more shame for me not to know," he says to himself. It is an example of how accurate poetic imagery can be.

Show don't tell: the old adage. It is what great poets do with economy and power; their relative freedom from the rules of syntax (sentence structure) or grammar, which confine prose writers, means images can bubble up through poetry in all kinds of extraordinary ways.

The second point worth making is that the pictures I came across don't just involve our sight. They involve other senses, too: *the noise of battle* (hearing), *chafing water* (touch – 'chafing' means rubbing). We might even imagine the smell of the *bloomy spray* and the *long grass*. When other senses are involved, we speak of **sensuous imagery**.

Some poems are made entirely of pictures. Here's one:

The Makings of Marmalade

unripe oranges in silk-lined sacks
sow-bristle brushes
china jugs of orange-washing water
one big bowl
pith-paring knives, one for each woman
a mountain of sugar, poured slowly
a small Sevillian well
songsheets against the tedium, in parts
pine cones for burning
silver spoons for licking up the lost bits
a seven-gallon pot
a waxed circle, a sellophane circle, elastic
small pieces of toast

(Gillian Allnutt, 1949 –)

This is as close to a painting as a poem can get, presenting an array of objects to the mind's eye. I'm not sure you could summarise the argument of this poem: there are no sentences for an argument to be worked out in. But it does awaken thoughts and feelings, as we imagine the women working meticulously in the hot Spanish (Sevillian) sun, singing songs to make the time pass.

It makes me think of all the labour that lies behind the marmalade on our toast. Poets across the ages have somehow transmuted the "sense impressions" of life and packaged them into words, but some are particularly, magically good.

Most of the images in "The Making of

Marmalade" are *concrete* images, with the poet giving us vivid impressions of *sow-bristle brushes* and *silver spoons for licking up the lost bits*. But when she describes the *mountain of sugar* she doesn't mean there is an actual mountain. She is using what is called **figurative** speech.

A simple test of a phrase if we're not sure is to ask: "Could it be literally true?" If the answer is no, then it's figurative. It's the language of the impossible. Figurative language can involve various figures of speech, of which by far the most important are **similes** and **metaphors**.

A simile makes an explicit comparison; a metaphor is implicit. In practice this means that a simile involves words such as *like* and *as*, while a metaphor by contrast says more directly that something *is* something else. When Wordsworth writes

> *I wandered lonely as a cloud*

he is using a simile. So is Matthew Arnold when he writes, in the lines quoted earlier:

> *...and afloat,*
> *And lonely as a truant child,*
> *In a waste wood, a single boat.*

But when Allnut writes about a *mountain of sugar* she is using a metaphor.

Similarly, Sylvia Plath is using a metaphor in her

poem "Blackberrying" when the speaker describes looking up at choughs (crow-like birds)

> *in black, cacophonous flocks –*
> *Bits of burnt paper wheeling in a blown sky...*

The comparison here gets its power from the idea that, in the speaker's imagination, the birds *are* wind-blown *Bits of burnt paper*.

Here are some metaphors from the quotes we looked at earlier:

> *The noise of battle roll'd*
> *a trug of thundercloud*
> *the sulk of a wet summer*
>
> (a trug is a kind of basket)

The metaphor is a remarkable device. It brings together in our mind things that would normally be separate – noise and the action of rolling, summer and sulking, a basket and a cloud. Each one is like a little lab experiment, turning two substances into a strange new one. Metaphors are part of normal speech: a storm of applause, a deep thought. The problem is they get over-used and worn out. But a fresh metaphor, in the right hands, can make the world new again.

When we find a metaphor or simile in a poem, we can ask what effect it has. If we were to analyse the metaphor of *the noise of battle roll'd,* for example, we might say it puts across the booming

Sylvia Plath at her typewriter. After her death by suicide in 1963, she was the first poet to be posthumously awarded a Pulitzer Prize

sound of the battle in a dramatic, memorable way: the sound seems like something solid, bouncing and bashing its way like a boulder through the mountains.

There's one further figure of speech we should look at before we move on, and that is **personification**. This describes an image where something non-human is given human qualities: *the angry storm, the sun peeped over the hilltops.* We've had at least one example in the poems we have looked at: Hardy complains *But Time, to make me grieve / Part steals, lets part abide*, painting old Father Time as a rather sadistic figure.

A FAMOUS MODERN IMAGE

In "The Love Song of J Alfred Prufrock", modernist poet
T S Eliot starts by leading us into what promises to be a
beautiful image of the evening; but then he twists it,
savagely, into an image which has become one of the most
famous lines in modern poetry:

> Let us go then, you and I,
> When the evening is spread out against the sky
> Like a patient etherised upon a table...

What's going on here? The first line is metrical; in other
words it has an even rhythm. It is quite sing-song, in fact.
We might expect a second line to go something like *When
the evening spreads the sky*. But our expectations are
confounded. Instead, the *lines themselves* spread out.
What we get is something like iambic pentameter (see
next section), but then in the third line the rhythm
becomes even more irregular. And it is that third line,
after the romantic allusion to an evening and sky, which
gives us the weird, puzzling image of a patient under
ether, meaning anaesthetic. Now, patients under
anaesthesia are not a common feature of love songs; nor

are they very popular as similes for sunsets. The poem has started in a normal, welcoming way – *Let us go* – and quite soon it has taken us somewhere very strange.

There's more to be said about the *patient etherised* image. For as well as being an anaesthetic, ether has another old sense: it can mean the clear sky, the upper region beyond the clouds, and that is important here, too. This is a modern picture, but one rooted in the past.

Even after the opening of the poem, we can start thinking about themes. A romantic promise (*Let us go...*) soon leads to this bleak picture of a patient on a table. Critics call this defamiliarisation: take something we're used to, like a sunset, and make it look new and strange. Painters do the same sort of thing. Paintings and poetic images can make us look at the world in a new way.

In the rest of the poem, and in T S Eliot's other writings, we find variations of the same thing: the experience of life comes over as complicated, fragmentary, hard to make sense of. In 'The Waste Land', we get a picture of the soul of modern man as sick, lost in a world which has lost its meaning and its magic. All of this was partly a response to a world which had been ripped to pieces by a world war ("Prufrock'" was published in 1917). And all of this vision of man and the world is embedded in the imagery. T S Eliot's poetry can be difficult. But then, as he pointed out, modern life, too, can be difficult, so poetry which tries to express modern life is bound to be complex and demanding. ∎

2. Sound

"Poetry begins, I dare say," T.S. Eliot once told an audience at Harvard, "with a savage beating a drum in a jungle." Eliot believed that when we first read a great poem it operates on us at a deeper level than words; it doesn't matter if we don't immediately understand it. When Eliot originally read Dante's "Inferno", he tells us, he read it in the original Italian before he had even learnt the language.

Sound and sense in poetry are always closely linked. Here is a poem by Tennyson:

The Eagle

He clasps the crag with crooked hands;
Close to the sun in lonely lands,
Ring'd with the azure world, he stands.
The wrinkled sea beneath him crawls;
He watches from his mountain walls,
And like a thunderbolt he falls.

A good way to appreciate the sound of this poem is to take a short phrase and let it work on us. *He clasps the crag.* On the word *clasps* with its bristling, clicking consonants I can feel the grip this great bird has on its stony perch. And in *crag*, the hard sounds capture the hard, jagged rock – a crag is like a *cliff or crevasse*. Reading the rest of the line, on *crooked* we feel the talons curling around the rock.

These repeated *c* consonants are **alliteration**.

But the word is less important than the effect the sounds have, helping us to imagine, to feel the scene physically. It's worth remembering that Tennyson didn't *have* to use these words: he could have said: *He holds the rock with spreading hands.* But the effect we've just been observing would have been lost. The *what* would be the same, but the *how* would be different, and so our experience would be different.

Another sound effect in these lines is the simple one of **rhyme**. Tennyson uses a triple rhyme, quite unusual in English: *hands, lands, stands.* One effect of this is to form a pattern which we find pleasing. Repetition gives a shape to things. And deep down we humans do seem to like shape, repetition, expecting something and then getting it after a little suspense-building wait. Rhyming speaks to our deep desire for order over disorder, pattern over chaos.

Reading Tennyson's poem, we become alert to the precise sounds and consider how they might relate to what the poem describes. For example, those words that end in *ands* are quite drawn out – a vowel, then an *n* which we can keep going, then moving over the *d* to the soft s: *la... n... ds.* If I think hard of the image and then say *lands* I can see a vast plain – *annn* – disappearing into the horizon of *ds.*

"Tennyson might not have meant that, you're reading far too much into it," you might say. But Tennyson thought *a lot* about sounds, and, even if he didn't think this exact thought, it is, in a sense, our poem as well as it is his. He wrote it; we're reading it.

Reading is itself a creative act – an act of discovery and interpretation, just as a pianist playing a Beethoven piece is making all sorts of interpretive decisions with the music the composer has given him.

To be technical: repetition of consonants is alliteration: *round the rough and ragged rocks rude and raucous rascals run.* Repetition of a final syllable (vowel plus consonants) is **rhyme**. Another kind of repetition is to repeat vowels. To spot this, you really have to listen in. But we find it in the lines above: *crag ... hands / Close... lonely / sea... beneath.* The repetition of vowel sounds is called **assonance**. The combined effect of alliteration, assonance and rhyme in these lines is to make us much more aware of the sounds of language than we normally are. They make the poetry into a piece of verbal music.

There are a couple of other technicalities to deal with, involving rhyme. The kind of rhyme Tennyson is using is called **full rhyme** – consonant and vowel sounds are repeated. But you'll also find rhymes, especially in modern poetry, which are wafer-thin:

> *It seemed that out of battle I escaped*
> *Down some profound dull tunnel, long since*
> *scooped*
> *Through granites which titanic wars had*
> *groined.*
> *Yet also there encumbered sleepers groaned ...*
> (Wilfred Owen, from "Strange Meeting")

In *escaped / scooped* we can see that the poet has

hung onto the consonant sounds but sort of twisted the vowel. Owen was a great experimenter with rhyme, and wanted to move away from the rather heavy effect that full final rhyme can create. The rhymes he uses are called **half rhymes** or **slant rhymes**. They are used a lot in modern poetry.

Many poets turned away from full rhymes in the early part of the 20th century. The horror of the First World War played its part in this; somehow the harmony we feel in proper rhyming would have seemed false to the poets caught up in the dreadful day-to-day carnage on the Western Front. Owen's use of half rhymes helps to create a sense of discord in his war poetry, of everything somehow being amiss and out of harmony.

Finally, we should consider the term **onomatopoeia**. This is used to describe words where the sounds seem remarkably close to the meaning: *Splash! Squelch!* Maybe *crag* could be called onomatopoeic, bundling up those hard *c* and *g* sounds. If we think we find a close resemblance between sound and sense we can suggest in our reading that there is an onomatopoiec effect. For example, at the end of Tennyson's poem, there's a pause after *thunderbolt*, then *he falls*. Whoosh! Light sounds and a short phrase to evoke the eagle hurtling down from his craggy perch. If you can explain *why* you're seeing or feeling that effect, then you're safe to call it onomatopoeia. And it's good spelling practice, too. It's not every day you write a word which has four vowels in a row.

3. Rhythm

Rhythm finds its way into language early in our lives, from the cooing and singing we received as babies, to clapping games in the playground, to nursery rhymes: ***Little Miss Muffet sat on a tuffet***...

The first thing we need to think about, in considering rhythm, is the **beat**. And to get to the beat, we need to think about syllables. **Beat** is stress, and in language stress falls on syllables. Syllables are what words break down into. In any word, there's a syllable that gets extra oomph, which is the **stressed** one:

Day = 1 syllable
To-**day** = 2
Yes-ter-day = 3
Im-**ag**-in-ing = 4
Im-ag-in-**a**-tion = 5

MASCULINE AND FEMININE RHYMES

The basic rhymes in English are known as *masculine* rhymes. This means they come in the last syllable of the line, as in William Blake's famous

poem, "Tyger Tyger":

> *When the stars threw down*
> *their spears*
> *And water'd heaven with*
> *their tears,*
> *Did He smile His work to*
> *see?*
> *Did He who made the lamb*
> *make thee?*

In masculine rhymes it is the last syllable of the line which is

You'll notice that each syllable has a vowel and one or more consonants stuck onto it: *To* = consonant *t* + vowel *o*. If you feel uncertain at this point, simply make lists of words of one, two, and three syllables, and highlight the stressed syllables. Those are the basic skills for everything that follows.

None of this is pure theory. We use stresses every day. Whenever we speak English, we stress some syllables over others, and emphasise important words. With a cheery smile, we say: "Good **mor**ning Mrs **Jones**, and **how** are **you** to**day**?" (If you say this with exactly equal stress on all the syllables, Mrs Jones will start crossing the street to avoid you.)

Rhythm emerges when we organise the beat syllables so they fall into a regular pattern, like objects on a shelf. This is a verse from the master Edward Lear's *Book of Nonsense*:

---

stressed (spears/tears; see/ thee).

So-called *feminine* rhymes are more subtle: they usually occur in words which have more than one syllable, with the second last syllable stressed and containing the rhyme sound; *greeting, retreating*; *dearly, nearly*; *master, plaster*; *Putney*; *chutney*. Feminine rhymes often showcase a poet's ingenuity: they bring words together in unusual combinations, as when W.H. Auden outlines his preference for a Midlands panorama over a Wordsworthian landscape in 'Letter to Lord Byron':

> *Clearer than Scafell Pike,*
> *my heart has stamped on*
> *The view from Birmingham*
> *to Wolverhampton.* ∎

There was an old person of Fife,
Who was greatly disgusted with life;
They sang him a ballad,
And fed him on salad,
Which cured that old person of Fife.

Now, having contemplated the wisdom in this poem, listen to the beats. If we say it aloud, pushing out the stresses, we get

*There **was** an old **per**son of **Fife**,*
*Who was **great**ly dis**gus**ted with **life**.*

The lines both have three stresses, fairly evenly

HAVING FUN WITH RYHMES

There are times when poets simply enjoy revelling in their rhyming skills. The famously suave and debonair Lord Byron loved to cut a dash in his poetry, as in these lines, with their mixture of masculine, feminine and, in the last couplet, half rhymes, which he scribbled in the margins of his masterpiece,

"Don Juan".

I would to heaven that I
*   were so much clay,*
As I am blood, bone,
* marrow, passion, feeling –*
Because at least the past
*   were passed away –*
And for the future – (but I
*   write this reeling,*
Having got drunk
*   exceedingly today,*
So that I seem to stand upon
*   the ceiling)*
I say – the future is a
*   serious matter –*
And so – for God's sake –
*   hock and soda water!*

placed. You can clap along to it, in even groups of three: *bom bom bom!* There follow a couple of lines of two stresses (*and* **sang** *him a* **ball***ad*), then a final one of three, giving a typical limerick formation of 3-3-2-2-3. And to add to the pattern, the three-stress lines are bound together by rhyme sound, and the middle two by another rhyme: *aabba*.

Here's the start of a poem by the Cornish writer Charles Causley:

Timothy Winters

Timothy Winters comes to school
With eyes as wide as a football-pool,

The poem is a cry to live in the moment, free from the consciousness of past and future. Its energy seems to fulfil that wish. There's clearly a very intricate rhyming structure at work here (a-b-a-b-a-b-c-c); at the same time the rhymes themselves often seem to fall into place just by chance. And the end of the stanza has a slightly tipsy feel to it, with its cry for *wine and water* undercutting the solemn claim that *the future is a serious matter.*

Look at the chain of rhymes that flows from *feeling.* The word is given prominence at the head of a list of earthly things Byron wants to rid himself of. It is not an easy word to rhyme on; but for Byron this difficulty becomes an opportunity to show his skill: the word *reeling* puts the skids under any temptation in us to believe too much in his *feeling* – and offers an apt description of what the verse does as it wheels from line to line; the next rhyme, on *ceiling,* is even bolder, revelling in the crazy, daring way with which it upturns any feeling we may have of lingering sincerity. Byron is having fun. The stanza is a party of sounds and wit. ■

Ears like bombs and teeth like splinters:
A blitz of a boy is Timothy Winters

Timothy Winters comes to school... four strong beats you can clap along to. And you can keep the clapping going through the next three lines, and the rest of the poem, too. *Bom bom bom bom.*

Notice, by the way, how Causley is using many of the other poetic devices we have looked at: rhyme (the lines here rhyme in pairs, so are called **rhyming couplets**), alliteration (***blitz of a boy***), simile (one each for eyes, ears, teeth), metaphor (*A blitz of a boy*). All of these are working together to put into our minds a big, dishevelled, powerful boy

You might think we've been making life easy for ourselves by sticking to easy stuff like limericks and children's verse. But so-called serious poetry follows just the same principles: after all, it's still words on a page. The thing, always, is to listen for the beat syllables. Let's look at, or rather listen to, some famous lines by Shakespeare:

*Shall **I** com**pare** thee **to** a **sum**mer's **day**?*
*Thou **art** more **love**ly **and** more **temp**er**ate**.*
*Rough **winds** do **shake** the **dar**ling **buds** of **May**,*
*And **sum**mer's **lease** hath **all** too **short** a **date**.*
(Sonnet 18)

Just as before, we find the same number of beats in each line, evenly spread. There were three in the limerick, four in "Timothy Winters", and now we

POETS ON POETRY

"I think it would be best described as the only possible reaction to a particular kind of experience, a feeling that you are the only one to have noticed something, something especially beautiful or sad or significant. [A poem is] a verbal device that will set off the same experience in other people, so that they too will feel How beautiful, how significant, how sad, *and the experience will be preserved. I suppose the kind of response I am seeking from the reader is* Yes, I know what you mean, life is like that.*"*
Philip Larkin on why he wrote poetry

"Poetry is a language in which man explores his own amazement."
Christopher Fry

"Genuine poetry can communicate before it is understood."
T.S. Eliot

"A poet's work is to name the unnameable, to point at frauds, to take sides, start arguments, shape the world, and stop it going to sleep." **Salman Rushdie**

"Poetry lies its way to the truth."
John Ciardi

"We make out of the quarrel with others, rhetoric, but of the quarrel with ourselves, poetry." **W.B. Yeats**

"A poem is like a shot of espresso – the fastest way to get a hit of mental and spiritual energy."
Jeanette Winterson

have gone up to five (which is usually the maximum in an English verse line, though there are some exceptions). And once again the lines are tied together by rhyme as well as rhythm; the rhyme here is in an *abab* pattern.

But you might sense some difference, too. The beats are not quite as "pushed out" as they are in the Causley poem. You might even query the stress I have put on little words like *to* and *and* in the first two lines. And you'd be right. When there are five stresses, one is often weaker than the others. Also, just labelling syllables as stressed and unstressed simplifies matters: there are *grades* of stress. If you say *Rough winds* you might find there's only a slight extra stress on *winds*, and the same with *too short*. So although there is a rhythmic frame, it isn't as obvious as in Causley's poem. It's a little like listening to classical music instead of pop. The beat is there, but it's not as clear.

The beat Shakespeare in his sonnets is writing to is a template of di-DUM, sometimes obviously, sometimes not so obviously, and sometimes taking a little break from it, then going back. Across this rhythm, lines will speed up and slow down, and there will be pauses in the middle of lines, sometimes marked by punctuation, sometimes not. It does take time to get used to it, but if you trust your ear and say it aloud you will get the hang of it. In literary criticism, this arrangement of beats is called **metre**.

Now there's no getting away from it. It's time to call in on the Department of Difficult Words.

Shakespeare, we noted, is writing to a template of di-DUM. He is using what is called an **iambic pentameter**, a term which sounds like it was designed to make a toothbrush seem as complicated as a space rocket. So please do this. Say the word, 'today': to**day**. Good. Now say 'today' five times. Congratulations! You have now produced a perfect iambic pentameter, as metrically regular as any line of English verse.

To explain this little miracle: the **iamb** is a bundle of two syllables, the first unstressed, the second stressed: di-DUM. And pentameter is just an old word for five (as in pentangle, or pentathlete).

> Rough **winds** do **shake** the **dar**ling **buds** of **May**
> to**day** to**day** to**day** to**day** to**day**.

Admittedly, *today today today today today* needs a bit of work before it becomes immortal verse, but the rhythm is steady. You can always go back to it to remind yourself what **iambic pentameter** means.

Now say *'morning'*. You have just uttered a **trochee**: DUM-di, *mor*ning. Say it four times, and you have come up with a **trochaic tetrameter**, four trochees. Trochee stands for the pair of syllables, tetrameter means four times. An iamb and a trochee are two kinds of metrical **foot**, the technical word for the two syllables bundled together. So we now have five technical terms:

Iamb: an unstressed syllable, then a stressed

one: *today, do **shake**, Peru*
Trochee: stressed-unstressed: ***morning, wonder***
Tetrameter: x 4
Pentameter: x 5
Foot: a repeated rhythmic pattern like an iamb or trochee

Note: **iamb** and **trochee** refer to arrangements of stressed and unstressed syllables, not words, so words can move across them: *I **won** | der **what** | I'll **do** | this **aft** | er**noon*** (iambic pentameter); ***rain**drops | **fall** up| **on** the | **window*** (trochaic tetrameter).

What we *shouldn't* do with these terms is just slap them on any poem we come across. We should use them, if they help, to get the rhythm of a piece of verse clear in our heads. In analysing the rhythm of verse, we are not in fact so interested in the regular lines as in the variations that poets make on them, and the effects they achieve with this.

Here are some lines from a 17th-century poem on the sad subject of a fawn being killed:

The Nymph Complaining for the Death of Her Faun

The wanton troopers riding by
Have shot my fawn, and it will die.
Ungentle men! They cannot thrive –
To kill thee! Thou ne'er didst alive
Them any harm …

(Andrew Marvell, 1621-1678)

52

William Blake's Ancient of Days. *Blake accompanied many of his poems with engravings, often involving religious imagary*

As ever, read for the meaning first: the nymph (forest girl) tells us that some men have shot her fawn, then speaks, lamentingly, to the fawn itself: *'To kill thee!'* (meaning *How could they!*). In what way is the poet organising the beats here? There's a fairly clear di-DUM rhythm, and four beats in a line, which makes it, technically, iambic tetrameter:

> The **wan**ton **troop**ers **rid**ing **by.**

What's more notable, though is where the poet departs from that, at the end:

> To **kill** thee! **Thou** ne'er **didst** alive
> **Them** any **harm** ...

The first line of this is regular, but the exclamation mark suggests a big pause (you can hear the nymph sobbing here). This pause is called a **caesura**. But the real shock to the metrical system comes in the next line. Instead of di-DUM we get a big stress: ***Them ..*** DUM! And of course that's what we would say: *You never did **them** any harm!* That variation, stressing *Them*, brings out the emotion of the moment. We were led to expect an iamb and we got a trochee. The Department of Difficult Words calls this variation – which is the most common in English metrical poetry – a **trochaic inversion**. And it's the regularity around the variation which gives it its power.

Rhythm is infinitely flexible. Long vowels and stressed syllables slow down the march of words:

> *I look into my glass*
> *And view my wasting skin*

is made of iambs, but as well as that, in those drawn-out syllables – *glass... view... waste* – with long vowels and prolonged consonants, we hear the weary, yearning voice of the speaker. It's iambic rhythm in first gear, the gear for slow viewing, pausing, meditating. Stress and speech sounds work together.

4. Structure

If we look back, once more, at the Hardy poem, we'll see that the verses all have a third line which is a bit longer than the others:

> *I look into my glass*
> *And view my wasting skin,*
> *And say, 'Would God it came to pass*
> *My heart had shrunk as thin.'*

And we notice, too, that the lines are tied together with rhyme. Hardy here is using a shape that comes up time and again in verse and songs: a first line, then a second line repeating or developing its idea, then a third line that reaches out like a hand in the dark, then a fourth that comes back and settles the verse to a close. "Happy birthday" has that shape, and so do hundreds of hymns. Bob Dylan's "Shelter from the Storm" follows exactly that pattern, verse after hypnotising verse. And so do countless other four-line verses. This shape, for statements in verse and song, is as familiar as a vase for flowers. And it affects the meaning: each verse or **stanza** is a statement, a reaching out, and a settling back. Without telling us, the speaker is composing his feelings as he is uttering them. The poem is not just about growing old, but feeling passions; it is about how we manage and contain the passions that rush through us. It is beautifully controlled and organised.

We humans are order-making creatures, leading, for the most part, structured existences. Our houses are divided into rooms, which are separated by walls. The sofa I'm looking at has two cushions, roughly equidistant. Poetry expresses the same need for arrangement. It is an ordering activity, giving shape to thoughts, feelings and arguments; and the shape is part of the meaning.

Poems find their shape in **lines** and **stanzas**. The following is a complete poem:

Parting at Morning

Round the cape of a sudden came the sea,
And the sun looked over the mountain's rim:
And straight was the path of gold for him*
And the need of a world of men for me.

(Robert Browning, 1812-1889)

*"him" refers to the sun

What can we say about how this poem is organised? Without even reading a word, we can confidently state that it is in four lines, in one group or **stanza**. In this case, it is a four-line verse called a **quatrain**. And the lines are grouped in a clear rhyme scheme of *abba*. Listening for the rhythm, we can hear four strong beats in each line, so we can say that the poem is organised into quite a regular metre (with slight variations, an iambic tetrameter).

There are other features worth noting. Each line contains a single **clause**, that is to say you could get out of each one a grammatical sentence that would make sense on its own. Lines 1 and 2 end with punctuation, marking off the clause. They are what we call **end-stopped**: lines 2,3 and 4 all start with 'And'.

We have identified the structure of the poem by line, stanza, metre, rhyme, and sentence; and we have noticed the little feature of **repetition** with that *And*. The next step is to link these observations to the meaning and effect. Reading the poem again, we find that it records a particular moment – the sea and the sun appearing to the speaker, presumably as he walks along. The last line is not easy, but it tells us that while the sun will trace his daily course – his *path of gold* – the speaker needs to return (from what?) to *the world of men*.

If there is a central tension here, it is between the rapture of the solitary speaker and his desire for the company of other humans. He cannot share the golden world of the sun. Perhaps the title, "Parting at Morning", gives us a clue, suggesting that he is parting from a beloved. But in any case this moment of revelation is what the poem records: the sight of the sun and sea in their splendour, followed by the speaker's reflection that he needs to get back to society.

The poem takes this experience, which must have happened in a flash, and structures it clearly so that we can follow it as a story: the sea appears (line 1), then the sun (2), then we think about the sun's path (3), then the man's path (4). Each line traces out a complete thought, chained by *and* to the next.

The structure gives a shape and a sense to the passing joy and impulse. And this shape makes it accessible to us: a scattering of sensations and feelings is turned into a calm series of statements. It builds up expectations – we wait for the rhyme sound to *sea* to appear, and we wait for the chain of statements to conclude in a full stop. The end of the poem resolves these expectations, bringing the reading to a satisfying close. Like Wordsworth remembering the daffodils, Browning remembers this moment in the morning and, in remembering, sorts it out into an ordered scheme. And with this ordering, the experience becomes visible and comprehensible to us.

Without this frame, the meaning and the feeling would vanish. Poems, like houses, need to be well built if they are to last.

5. Line endings

Now let us return to a poem we looked at earlier:

The Sick Rose

O Rose thou art sick.
The invisible worm
That flies by night
In the howling storm:

Has found out thy bed
Of secret joy:
And his dark secret love
Does thy life destroy.

This poem is in eight lines, grouped in two quatrains. Like Browning's, it is bound together by metre, with two strong beats in the line, falling on two key words: *O **Rose** thou art **sick***. There is rhyme, but only on the second and fourth lines.

There are two main differences between Blake's poem and Browning's: first, Blake's lines are short; secondly, they do not correspond with clauses (a clause is a statement that could stand as a sentence on its own). Lines 2 and 3 are not end-stopped, nor are lines 5 and 7; and the punctuation is odd. The colon at the end of the first verse breaks up the sentence and seems to be there to make us pause for a moment. It comes a surprise to realise that the whole poem is made up of just two sentences.

So why set it out like this? One answer is that the short lines focus our attention: *The invisible worm* stands out because it is given a whole line to itself. This is a poem we are clearly intended to read phrase by phrase, taking our time over each one. Another effect is that the short, two-stress lines form a pattern we expect, so when it is broken and we get *three* stressed key words in *dark secret love* there is a real drama to it: here, we sense, is where the core of the poem lies.

After the first line, the lines also run into each other as the sentence unwinds. This is a device called **enjambment**, French for "striding". We can say that *The invisible worm / That flies by night* is an instance of enjambment, but we are not saying anything interesting until we suggest what the *effect* of that is. Here, I suggest, there is a kind of double motion: we pause on *worm* because it is the end of the line, and a key and intriguing word, but we also feel the need to read on from it to make sense. The enjambment places emphasis on the line ending. And it creates a sense of suspense: we pause on an image before it develops into something bigger.

It is usually the case that the more sentences move across line endings, the greater the effect of turbulence, of the mind making an effort to arrange thoughts, sensations and feelings. It's interesting that while Browning is writing about his experience in the past tense, Blake is in the present. The moment of finding the sick rose is happening *now*: the poem is a record of the effort to capture this vision as it occurs to him.

Sometimes poets use enjambments to surprise us, as in these lines by Wordsworth's near-contemporary, Thomas Lovell Beddoes, spoken by a character in his play *Death's Jest-Book*:

> *I could not wish him in my rage to die*
> *Sooner...*

The first line tricks us. The poet is saying: *However furious I am, I wouldn't want him to die*. We think Beddowes is about to add something generous. But he doesn't: lurking round the corner of the line is the word *Sooner*, which creates a last-minute twist of the knife. He is saying not that he *doesn't* want the man to die but that he *does* (though not too soon).

Here are the first few lines of a famous poem by W.H. Auden called "Musee des Beaux Arts":

> *About suffering they were never wrong,*
> *The Old Masters: how well they understood*
> *Its human position; how it takes place*
> *While someone else is eating or opening a*
>   *window or just walking dully along...*

Auden is telling us how the great painters of the past, the Old Masters, understood the truth about human suffering – how it is very intense, making us feel we should take it seriously, yet happens while most of us are busily getting on with our everyday lives and paying no attention. That is the central conflict of the poem.

The tone is casual and chatty. Look at the way the poem starts. The obvious way of starting would have been:

> *The Old Masters were never wrong about*
> *suffering.*

But Auden instead changes the natural word order, or syntax, and *reverses* the two phrases, making his opening line much more interesting and giving emphasis to the crucial word *suffering*, with its three heavy syllables, by placing it so early.

> *About suffering, they were never wrong*

And just as Blake makes us wait after the word *worm*, Auden then adds a small, extra sense of drama by making us wait to know who *they* are – the people who were never wrong. We have a moment of suspense at the end of the line before we learn the truth.

> *About suffering, they were never wrong,*
> *The Old Masters...*

It's a classic example of the use of enjambment. As the critic Terry Eagleton has put it, we have "to step across the line-ending to find out exactly who was never wrong about suffering". And the poem's "air of well-bred worldliness" – as if we're hearing from someone who's seen a lot and is quietly giving us his reflections on life – is kept up by the constant use of enjambments and the mixture of short lines and long ones. So suffering, we're told, takes place

While someone else is eating or opening a
window or just walking dully along...

This is a stumbling, untidy line; there seem to be too many words in it; the poet is perhaps suggesting that

QUEEN ELIZABETH'S TROUBLED HEART

Endstopping often supports an effort to impose order, as in these thoughts by Elizabeth I on a man whose attentions she rejected:

I grieve and dare not show
my discontent,
I love and yet am forced to
seem to hate,
I do, yet dare not say I ever
meant,
I am stark mute but
inwardly do prate.
I am and am not, I freeze
and yet am burned,

Since from myself
another self I turned.

The Queen's emotions may be muddled, but in the verse she tries, literally, to get her feelings into line, neatly fulfilling a much later definition W. H. Auden gave of poetry as "the clear expression of mixed feelings".

See how each line holds two contradictory emotions alongside one another – grief and composure, love and hate, silence and inward torment – before the passage reaches a climax as *two* conflicting impulses are crowded together in its second last line. The verse, then, clarifies the Queen's feelings: whether writing it helped her to triumph over her turmoils or just made them worse is open to question. ∎

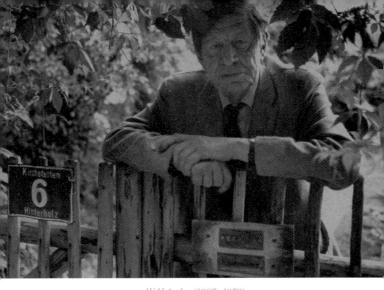
W H Auden (1907 - 1973)

the line is a bit like life itself – all those experiences we have piling up, one on top of the other, while elsewhere there is suffering going on which, most of the time, we're not aware of. That, so the poet seems to say, is just the way things are.

Yet although the Auden poem is less formal in its structure than either Blake's or Browning's, it is carefully designed – though in a way which makes us think it isn't. It even rhymes, very discreetly ("wrong"/ "along"), with the enjambments making it hard to spot the rhymes as the thoughts flow freely on from one line to the next.

Many modern poems use form in a similarly subtle way. Take this one by Moniza Alvi:

Exile

The old land swinging in her stomach
she must get to know this language
better – key words, sound patterns
wordgroups of fire and blood.

Try your classmates with
the English version of your name.
Maria. Try it.
Good afternoon. How are you?

I am fine. Your country –
you see it in a drop of water.
The last lesson they taught you there
was how to use a gun.

And now in stops and starts
you grow a second city in your head.
It is Christmas in this school.
Sarajevo is falling through

a forest of lit-up trees,
cards and decorations.
Mountains split with gunfire
swallow clouds, birds, sky.

Here we can tell at a glance that the poem is organised into quatrains. The line lengths, though roughly equal, vary. There is no regular rhyme scheme and no regular metre to establish where lines should begin and end.

Enjambments can create little pauses and surprises which would be lost in prose.

> *Try your classmate with*
> *The English version of your name.*

Could this be a teacher speaking? Is the little suspenseful pause after *with* capturing the teacher thinking for a second of a challenge to give the girl? Endings and spaces can suggest the pauses and movements we might make if we were performing the poem to an audience.

Later in the poem there is an enjambment between stanzas: *Sarajevo is falling through // a forest of lit-up trees.* Here, the gap on the page between the stanzas seems to suggest the stream of memory, and helps us to realise, I think, that the girl is seeing two things at the same time: the terrible destruction of her home city, and the decorated Christmas tree in front of her. The *lit-up trees* are her childish description of the Christmas trees, but they also bring to mind the image of explosions and gunfire. We wouldn't catch that double image if we weren't pausing for balance on each stepping stone of the poem.

We can only speculate. Of course it is possible that we will see things the poet did not intend, but a possible answer to that thought, as we observed earlier, is that the writer and the reader *collaborate* in a poem.

Conclusion

We have now considered *what* poems are saying, and *how* they say them. In English Literature studies, the kind of careful reading we have been attempting is called Practical Criticism. In its purest form, Practical Criticism goes no further than this: we make what we can of the words on the page, without referring to history books or biographies or any other background material. It is like looking at a picture in an art gallery with no idea of where it came from or even who painted it. And we can enjoy most poems without knowing anything at all about their creator.

All the same, it's not just interesting but helpful to know something about the poets we read. The knowledge can help us make connections between poetry and the world from which it emerges.

Poets in the 14th century, to take an obvious example, wrote very different poetry from the poets of today. This isn't just a matter of the language changing. They had other things on their mind, such as the Black Death, the huge power of the Church, the Last Judgement, and the best route to Canterbury. Their poetry belongs in that world, which we call its **context**.

And while we don't need to know the background to a poem to find it moving, our experience of it can take on an extra depth if we ask questions about where it comes from – how it connects with the poet's life, with other writings of the period, or with the wider world of culture, society and politics.

Reading Wordsworth's "I wandered lonely as a cloud", for example, might make us curious about its author. Soon enough we will find out that he lived up in Cumbria (his house, Dove Cottage, is now a museum). It's interesting that the sighting of daffodils described in the poem actually happened: we can read another description of the event in the journal of William's sister, Dorothy (Thursday 15th April, 1802):

> I never saw daffodils so beautiful they grew
> among the mossy stones about and about them,
> some rested their heads upon these stones as on a
> pillow for weariness and the rest tossed and
> reeled and danced ...

So the two must have discussed it. Which was the first to think the daffodils looked as if they were dancing, I wonder? If we read more of Wordsworth's poetry, we find the main subject of this poem – how events live in the memory, and the effect these memories have – was very important to him. His great autobiographical work *The Prelude* examines the way that his emotions were shaped by his childhood in Cumbria. Wordsworth believed profoundly that nature was itself a great teacher, and that "The Child is father of the Man".

His deep interest in nature, and in what we feel, links him to the movement historians call Romanticism, and to fellow writers, artists and thinkers who in their work explored similarly powerful feelings and the lessons they can teach us. Knowing a little about Wordsworth's life, and his beliefs, deepens our experience of his poetry.

As to *why* poets write poetry – well, sometimes they tell us what they are trying to do. Wordsworth, whose poetry is striking for its egalitarianism – his belief that we are all equal – said he wrote partly to show that men who do not wear fine clothes can feel deeply. Milton ambitiously sets out in *Paradise Lost* to "justify the ways of God to man"; Wilfred Owen tell us he feels a duty to pass on the reality of what it was like to fight on the Western Front: "all a poet can do today is warn".

At other times, we can shrewdly guess that a poem is meant to persuade us to think or feel something. Or we simply take a poem as an invitation to look at things in a new way, to widen our vision of the world. But whatever our approach, we go on listening to the ghosts – and enjoying and contemplating the messages they send us.

THE SONNET

English poems come in all shapes and sizes, from little couplets to vast epics.

Some forms suit certain kinds of material: the ballad is handy for telling stories; blank verse (unrhymed iambic pentameter), with its room for varied sentences and speech rhythms, suits the dramatic poetry of Shakespeare.

One form which keeps coming up in English verse is the 14-line sonnet. Imported from Italy in the 16th century, this became the verse form of choice for many love poets. A little too long for a short lyrical outburst, but too short for a story, the sonnet seems perfect for a little internal drama, a thought going for a walk.

There are two main kinds of sonnet, the Italian and the English. The Italian sonnet divides into an **octave** (a group of eight lines) which rhymes *abbaabba*, and a **sestet** (six lines) which makes various patterns out of *cde* rhymes. The point where the octave meets the sestet is called the **volta**, meaning "turn", and it is often here that the sonnet "turns" by taking us in a new direction.

Remember me when I am gone away,
Gone far away into the silent land;
When you can no more hold me by the hand,
Nor I half turn to go yet turning stay.
Remember me when no more day by day
You tell me of our future that you planned;
Only remember me; you understand

It will be late to counsel then or pray.
Yet if you should forget me for a while
And afterwards remember, do not grieve:
For if the darkness and corruption leave
A vestige of the thoughts that once I had,
Better by far you should forget and smile
Than that you should remember and be sad.

(Christina Rossetti)

This poem packs a powerful punch in a short space: it's like a voice from the grave, allowing the bereaved to "move on" and be happy. And it gains part of its power from being very tightly organised. That tightness adds to its intensity. We notice that the octave divides into two **quatrains**, each ending in a full stop:

Remember me when I'm not here any more.

The second quatrain is a variation on that:

Remember me when I'm not here to speak to.

We notice, too, that the lines are largely end-stopped: the speaker is firmly in control of what she is saying. The form demands control: *abbaabba* is a tough discipline, requiring the poet to find four *a* and four *b* sounds, without any of them appearing forced. That's much harder to do in English than Italian.

After line eight comes the **volta**, and here we get a signal of a new direction with the word *Yet*, followed by the reassuring message that it's all right to forget sometimes, that the main thing is to hold on to what was good, and be happy rather than permanently mournful: *Remember me.... but* is the basic outline of the argument.

The rhyme scheme for the sestet here is *cddece*. The six lines follow a line of thought as it works itself out in the last line and concludes with the third and last full stop of the poem. The Italian sonnet is sometimes also called the Petrarchan sonnet, because it was much used by the medieval Italian poet Petrarch.

The English sonnet also has an octave and a sestet, but the rhyme scheme is different: *ababcdcdefefgg*. Seven rhyme sounds, rather than five, with none needed more than twice. This form is also called the Shakespearean sonnet, as it's particularly associated with him. So let's take an example from Shakespeare. Here he is making fun of the kind of love sonnets that were fashionable at the time, with their lavish praise – in imitation of Petrarch – of the lady's beauties:

> *My mistress' eyes are nothing like the sun;*
> *Coral is far more red than her lips' red;*
> *If snow be white, why then her breasts are dun;*
> *If hairs be wires, black wires grow on her head.*
> *I have seen roses damask'd, red and white,*
> *But no such roses see I in her cheeks;*
> *And in some perfumes is there more delight*
> *Than in the breath that from my mistress reeks:*
> *I love to hear her speak, yet well I know*
> *That music hath a far more pleasing sound;*
> *I grant I never saw a goddess go,*
> *My mistress when she walks treads on the ground.*

And yet by heaven I think my love as rare
As any she belied with false compare.

Again we have a full stop or heavy pause at the end of each quatrain of the octave. The octave is made up of short sentences (unlike Rossetti's): the first four end-stopped lines are all complete clauses. Over these eight lines, Shakespeare is really repeating, with variations, a single idea: *my* beloved is nothing like these ridiculous idealised pictures you read about.

We then expect the volta, but there is no "turn" here. The poet simply continues the same line of thought: *her* speech isn't like music; she doesn't float like a goddess.

This is quite common in the English sonnet: instead of octave and sestet we get three quatrains (*ababcdcdefef*) leading to a final **rhyming couplet**. And it's here that we find the volta, signalled by the same word Rossetti used: "And *yet*". We've been kept waiting for that "yet" over 12 lines. The couplet here means:

I think my love's as precious as any woman who is lied about with false comparisons (any she means any woman)

The couplets at the end of Shakespeare's sonnets are put to all sorts of uses, from the delayed volta here, to a concluding nugget of proverbial wisdom. The Romantic poet John Keats preferred the Italian sonnet because he thought the English one was weighed down by that last couplet. On the other hand, the Italian sonnet, with its strict octave rhyme scheme, can sound a little stiff.

A SHORT HISTORY OF ENGLISH VERSE

Old English (700 to 1100)

English starts with the arrival of the Angles and Saxons in the fifth century AD, following the departure of the Romans. Their Germanic languages merged to form Anglo-Saxon, aka Old English, and the earliest writing in it dates from about 700. Old English looks like a foreign language today. The most famous Old English poem is *Beowulf*, a heroic epic with monsters and dragons set in the old Germanic lands. Seamus Heaney's recent translation is a great read.

Middle English (1100 to 1500)

In 1066, the Normans invaded and occupied England. With them came a stock of French words, which mingled with Old English and gradually transformed the language.

Middle English is easier to read than Old English, and the later 14th century is a particularly rich period, with Chaucer's *Troilus and Criseyde* and *The Canterbury Tales* giving us a lively portrait of the medieval world. In the same period William Langland wrote an extraordinary portrait of contemporary life, *Piers Plowman* – passionate, visionary, and angry. And the anonymous "Gawain poet" wrote

Gawain and the Green Knight and *Pearl*, both of which can be read in brilliant translations by Simon Armitage.

Early Modern (1500-1700)

This period includes the Renaissance, when new ideas from the continent, and new learning derived from the study of the classics, poured into English culture.

In the mid-1500s the sonnet appears in its English form; its early practitioners included Edmund Spenser, Sir Philip Sidney and William Shakespeare. (Spenser also wrote the vast *Faerie Queene* (1590-96) which describes the adventures of Arthur's knights, all in an elaborate praise of Queen Elizabeth I, who paid Spenser a £50 pension for his pains, although there is no evidence she ever read it.)

The Renaissance, though, is most famous for its dramatic verse: it was the time of Marlowe (*Dr Faustus*) and Ben Jonson (*The Alchemist*) as well, of course, as Shakespeare, who wrote not just his plays but also two long narrative poems, "Venus and Adonis" and "The Rape of Lucrece". The early 1600s saw the emergence of the so-called 'Metaphysical' poets – in particular John Donne, George Herbert and Andrew Marvell, who wrote poems which are passionate, clever and formally ingenious.

The English Renaissance is often thought to end with John Milton's mighty epic in blank verse, *Paradise Lost* (first version, 1667) – telling the story of Adam and Eve's expulsion from the Garden of Eden – and with his near-contemporary John Dryden, whose "Annus Mirabilis" (1667) combines narrative, description, inventive imagery and controlled form.

Restoration poetry at the end of the 17th century – following the end of Cromwell's Republic and the restoration to the throne of Charles 11 – is marked by a reaction against the puritanism of writers like Milton and a relish for the pleasures of the good life, particularly love and sex. The Earl of Rochester is perhaps the best known, and certainly the most notorious, of these Cavalier courtly poets.

The 18th Century

A good deal of 18th-century poetry is poised, and witty, making sharp observations of the world. This is especially true of Alexander Pope, England's greatest satirical poet, who loved rhyming couplets and is most famous for *The Rape of the Lock*. Other well-known 18th-century poems include Thomas Gray's "Elegy, Written in a Country Churchyard" and Samuel Johnson's "The Vanity of Human Wishes".

The late 18th century sees the dawn of the Romantic movement, with its greater emphasis on personal feeling: the Scottish poet Robert Burns published a selection of his lyrics, The Kilmarnock Volume, in 1786. William Blake's *Songs of Innocence and Experience* (1789-94) deals with the passage of human life and at the same time attacks social injustices of the time.

Early 19th Century: The Romantics

The English Romantics were above all concerned with celebrating nature and the human imagination. The French Revolution of 1789, with its overthrowing of the old order, was a hugely important moment for the

Romantics. The "first generation" Romantics were William Wordsworth and Samuel Taylor Coleridge, who, in their introduction to *Lyrical Ballads* (1798), declared their aim of stripping poetry of ornament and returning it to the language and subjects of ordinary life.

The second generation romantics were Byron, Keats and Shelley. Byron wrote intense lyrics but also satirical and narrative verse. Shelley and Keats composed intense and passionate lyric poetry about human feeling and imagination. All three died tragically young. Somewhat apart from the Romantics is the poet John Clare, whose work brings to vivid life the countryside and its people and customs.

Later 19th Century: The Victorians

Following the Romantics came a period of great stylistic variety, under the reign of Queen Victoria (1837-1901). The huge output of Alfred, Lord Tennyson ranges from long narrative poems to short lyrics. His long poem *In Memoriam* (1849), written for a dead friend, is a notable elegy, full of the thoughts that haunted the Victorian mind. Robert Browning developed the dramatic monologue in *Men and Women* (1855). Female poets such as Emily Brontë and Christina Rossetti developed their own styles and forms. The 19th century was also a great age for nonsense verse, in the hands of Lewis Carroll and Edward Lear.

The 20th Century

Among the greatest poets of the early 20th century is Thomas Hardy, who considered himself more a poet than a novelist. His lyric poems are notable for their range of form and their depth of feeling, none more so than the poems he wrote remembering his first wife Emma. This period also saw the poets of the First World War of 1914-18: Wilfred Owen and Siegfried Sassoon are the best known. Edward Thomas, who also served, and died, in the war, was prompted to write poetry by his friend the American poet Robert Frost: his work, composed in a short period, presents an intense contemplation of England and the English countryside. Another great poet of the early 20th century is W B Yeats, the first Irishman to win the Nobel Prize for literature, which was awarded to him in 1923.

The period following World War One saw the emergence of the modernist movement, its most famous exponent (in the field of poetry) being T.S. Eliot. Eliot wrote what is probably the most famous poem of the 20th century, *The Waste Land*, in 1922. Modernist poetry is often fragmented, unpredictable, and difficult, its form intended to capture and reflect the bewildering nature of modern experience.

As literature moves closer to us in time, it becomes harder to see particular patterns. But one way of reading later poets is in the light of the influence of earlier giants like Hardy and Eliot. Hardy's use of set verse forms is continued by W H Auden, best known for his poetry of the 1930s, which describe an uncertain period, with the next war looming. Like Hardy, Auden writes in a way which seems conversational and approachable, not deliberately obscure. Philip Larkin was also inspired by Hardy, capturing wry, rather downbeat experiences in rhymed and metrical verse forms. After him, James Fenton, Don Paterson, Glyn Maxwell and Simon Armitage are among those who have continued to use traditional verse to write about contemporary concerns.

The tradition of Modernism, on the other hand, has been continued by writers like Basil Bunting, and later Geoffrey Hill, whose complex and demanding work records a tense and tough engagement with a range of issues, particularly our relationship to history.

Poetry today

At the start of the 21st century, with English established as a global language, the variety of cultures and identities to which English poetry gives expression has never been greater. We have already seen examples of the range of female writers (Alice Oswald), and of postcolonial writing (John Agard, Moniza Alvi). The work of the great Seamus Heaney, from its base in rural Northern Ireland, ranges over great territories of history, memory and experience. Recent poet laureates Andrew Motion and Carol Ann Duffy have been much concerned with introducing young people to poetry and making sure it has a place in normal lives. Poet-performers like Benjamin Zephaniah and Kate Tempest give poetry a vibrant place in public spaces. Poetry, in short, continues to speak to us in many tongues, and many voices.

FURTHER READING

A good way to get into reading poetry is to find an anthology that appeals to you. There are hundreds of anthologies of poems – selected by period, subject, country and so on – and new ones coming out all the time. Here are some favourites:

Anthologies

The Rattle Bag, edited by Seamus Heaney and Ted Hughes (London: Faber, 1982)

The School Bag, edited by Seamus Heaney and Ted Hughes (London: Faber, 1997)

Two chunky anthologies by two of the greatest poets of the twentieth century. Open them at random and you'll make some great discoveries.

Staying Alive (Newcastle: Bloodaxe Books, 2002) and *Being Alive* (2004), both edited by Neil Astley, bring together a wonderful collection of mainly modern poems exploring all sorts of corners of life.

The Oxford Book of English Verse, edited by Christopher Ricks (Oxford: Oxford University Press, 1999). A historical anthology, presenting poems in chronological order.

Books about Poetry

Books which introduce poetry to children are valuable and inspirational. All of these take us to the nub of the matter:

Georgia Heard, *For the Good of the Earth and Sun: Teaching Poetry* (London: Heinemann, 1999)

Ted Hughes, *Poetry in the Making* (London: Faber, 1967)

Kenneth Koch, *Making Your Own Days:The Pleasures of Reading and Writing Poetry* (New York: Pocket Books, 1999)

Michael Rosen, *What is Poetry: The Essential Guide to Reading and Writing Poems* (London: Walker Books, 2016)

More advanced
Here are some more academic guides, which introduce a wide range of terms and ideas:

Terry Eagleton, *How to Read a Poem* (New York: John Wiley &Sons, 2006)

Stephen Fry, *The Ode Less Travelled* (London: Arrow, 2007). Plenty here on metre and form

John Hollander, *Rhyme's Reason* new, enlarged edition (London and New Haven: Yale University Press, 1989). Brilliant little book, introducing verse forms with original examples.

John Lennard, *The Poetry Handbook* (Oxford: Oxford University Press, 1996).

John Peck and Martin Coyle, *Practical Criticism* (Basingstoke: Palgrave, 1985)

Peter Sansom, *Writing Poems* (Newcastle: Bloodaxe Books, 1994)

Jeffrey Wainwright, *Poetry: The Basics* (London: Routledge, 2011)

Readings. The following provide close readings of individual poems.

Ruth Padel, *52 Ways of Looking at a Poem* (London: Vintage, 2002) and *The Poem and the Journey* (London: Chatto and Windus, 2007). Really helpful on understanding modern and contemporary poetry

Camille Paglia, *Break Blow Burn* (New York: Vintage Books USA, 2006)

Carol Rumens, Poem of the Week for The Guardian online.

Poets on Poetry
Unsurprisingly, poets themselves have written some of the most useful books on poetry. Among them are:

James Fenton, *An Introduction to English Poetry* (London: Viking, 2002)

Glyn Maxwell, *On Poetry* (London: Oberon, 2012)

Mary Oliver, *A Poetry Handbook* (Harcourt, 1994)

Ezra Pound, *ABC of Reading* (London: Faber, 1951)

Rainer Maria Rilke, *Letters to a Young Poet*, translated by Charlie Routh (London: Penguin, 2012)

Films

Poetry doesn't make good blockbuster material, but these are all well worth watching for their insights.

Bright Star (2009) Beautiful film about John Keats and his love for Fanny Brawne.

Dead Poets Society (1989) Cheesy, perhaps, but irresistible film about an unconventional English teacher in a traditional private school in America. (I'm unconvinced, though, that destroying books we disagree with is the way forward.)

Howl (2010) About Allen Ginsberg's long poem 'Howl', which was put on trial for obscenity.

Il Postino (1994) Beautiful Italian film about a venerable poet, based on the Chilean writer Pablo Neruda, and his friendship with a Sicilian postman.

Elsewhere, poetry has a foothold in the radio in programmes like Roger McGough's excellent *Poetry, Please*; and occasionally a programme on a poet will surface on television. There are many poetry websites, among the most established Poetry Archive (which includes recordings), and the American site Poetry Foundation.

But in the end it comes down to books. An old, yellowing out-of-print volume in a second-hand bookshop might be just what you're looking for ... Happy reading.

Afterword

Experiencing poetry is a collaboration between writer and reader, and writing about it extends the principle of collaboration further. I'm grateful to Andrew Hodgson for excellent material to work from in several sections of the book; to Caroline Moore for further contributions; to Paul Woodward for meticulous work on production; to Louisa Thomas for correcting proofs; and to Jolyon Connell for suggesting the project in the first place, and shepherding it to publication.

Notes

CG CONNELL GUIDES

Concise, intelligent guides to history and literature

CONNELL GUIDES TO LITERATURE

NEW: CONNELL GUIDES TO HISTORY

"Connell Guides should be required reading in every school in the country."
Julian Fellowes, creator of Downton Abbey

*'What Connell Guides do is bring immediacy and clarity: brevity with
depth. They unlock the complex and offer students an entry route."*
Colin Hall, Head of Holland Park School

"These guides are a godsend. I'm so glad I found them."
Jessica Enthoven, A Level student, St Mary's Calne

To buy any of these guides, or for more information, go to
www.connellguides.com
Or contact us on (020)79932644 / info@connellguides.com

First published in 2017 by
Connell Guides
Spye Arche House
Spye Park
Lacock
Wiltshire
SN15 2PR

10 9 8 7 6 5 4 3 2 1

'Body' © Alice Oswald
'The Makings of Marmalade' © Gillian Allnutt
'Exile' © Moniza Alvi

Picture credits:

p.16 © Getty Images
p.37 © REX Features
p.64 © Getty Images

A CIP catalogue record for this book is available from the British Library.
ISBN 978-1-907776-66-3

Design © Nathan Burton

Assistant Editors:
Brian Scrivener and Paul Woodward

Printed in Malta

www.connellguides.com